THE WORLD'S BIGGEST MACHINES

Marcie Aboff

Raintree

www.raintreepublishers.co.uk
Visit our website to find out
more information about
Raintree books.

To order:
☎ Phone 0845 6044371
🖷 Fax +44 (0) 1865 312263
🖳 Email myorders@raintreepublishers.co.uk

Customers from outside the UK please telephone +44 1865 312262

Raintree is an imprint of Capstone Global Library Limited,
a company incorporated in England and Wales having its
registered office at 7 Pilgrim Street, London, EC4V 6LB
– Registered company number: 6695582

Edited by Nancy Dickmann and Megan Cotugno
Designed by Jo Hinton-Malivoire
Picture research by Tracy Cummins
Originated by Capstone Global Library
Printed and bound in China by CTPS

ISBN 978 1 406216 86 8 (hardback)
15 14 13 12 11
10 9 8 7 6 5 4 3 2 1

ISBN 978 1 406219 71 5 (paperback)
16 15 14 13 12
10 9 8 7 6 5 4 3 2 1

British Library Cataloguing in Publication Data
Aboff, Marcie.
The world's biggest machines. -- (Extreme machines)
629'.046-dc22
A full catalogue record for this book is available from the
British Library.

Acknowledgments
We would like to thank the following for permission to
reproduce photographs: Alamy pp. **14** (© Eric Glenn),
15 (© INTERFOTO); AP Images p. **11** (THE CANADIAN
PRESS/Larry MacDougal); Corbis pp. **4** (© Juan Carlos
Ulate/Reuters), **6** (© Neville Elder), **13** (© YONHAP/
epa), **18** (© JOE SKIPPER/Reuters), **20** (© BAZUKI
MUHAMMAD/Reuters), **23** (© Yogi, Inc); Getty Images
pp. **12** (Munshi Ahmed/Bloomberg), **19** (Joe Raedle), **21**
(Lester Lefkowitz), **22** (Time Life Pictures); istockphoto
p. **24**; Krøll Cranes A/S p. **25**; Landov pp. **5** (DAVID
GRAY/Reuters), **10** (Norm Betts), **17** (Kyodo); Mosterlimo.
com pp. **8**, **9** (Bob Fisher); NASA pp. **26** (Troy Cryder),
27; Shutterstock p. **7** (© Michael Stokes); U.S. Navy p. **16**
(Airman Natalia E. Panetta).

Cover photograph of the crawler transporter from
Kennedy Space Center, FL produced with permission of
NASA (Kennedy Space Center (NASA-KSC).

Some words are shown in bold, **like this**. You can find
out what they mean by looking in the glossary.

Contents

Big machines

Some machines are big, and others are really big. They make a car look like a toy! They carry aeroplanes, build tall buildings, and move rockets. If you see one coming towards you, get out of the way!

↑ Don't get caught behind these giant mining trucks!

Bigfoot monster truck

Bigfoot is a huge monster truck. Monster trucks are like pickup trucks. Contests are held to see which is the toughest. With tyres that are 3 metres tall, Bigfoot rolls straight over cars, crushing them easily.

How big?
4.7 metres tall

6

EXTREME FACT
Bigfoot was the first truck to jump over a 727 jumbo jet!

MonsterLimo

MonsterLimo is the longest monster truck. Inside, there are leather seats, coloured lights, and surround sound music. It is also high off the ground. You have to climb up stairs to get in. Some cars could drive right under it!

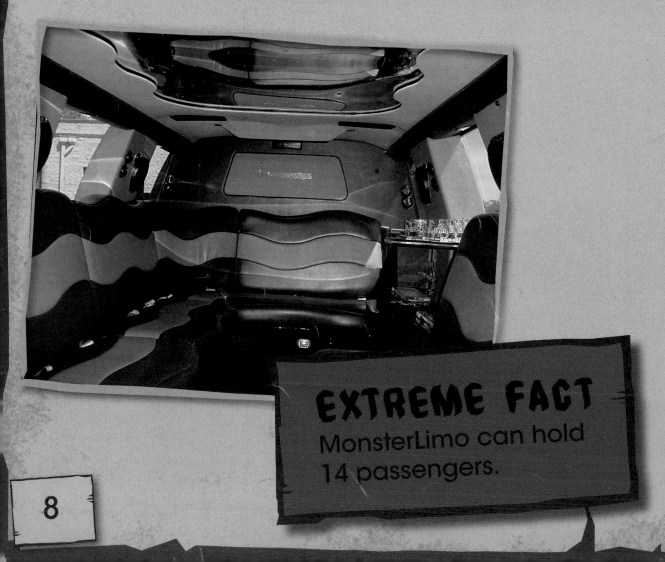

EXTREME FACT

MonsterLimo can hold 14 passengers.

How big?
10 metres long

↑ MonsterLimo is stretched out!

Caterpillar 797 truck

One of the largest dumper trucks in the world is the Caterpillar 797. This powerful machine is made for big **mining** and **construction** projects. It can hold 363 tonnes. The tyres are over 4 metres tall!

stairway and ladder

You need to climb a stairway or ladder just to get inside this truck!

How big?
7.3 metres tall

128

CAT

11

Airbus A380

Airbus A380 is a giant jumbo jet. This special double-decker aeroplane is the largest **passenger** aeroplane in the world. The planes have snack bars and lounges. Some even have full-size beds and showers!

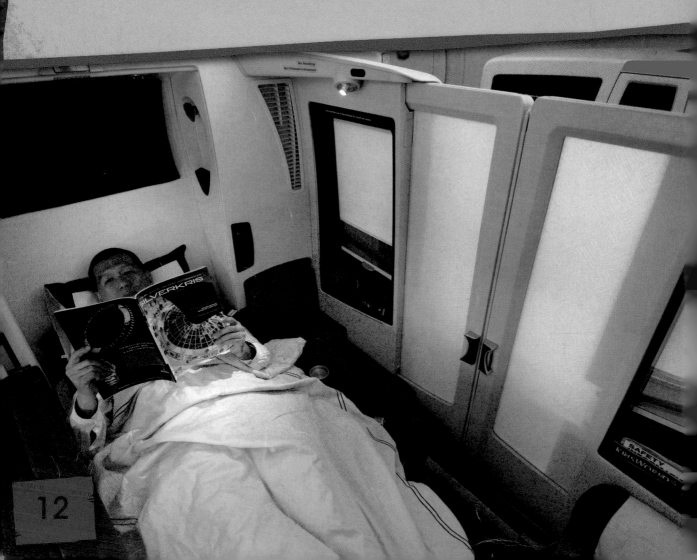

How big?
72.5 metres long

EXTREME FACT
Some Airbus planes can
seat 500 passengers!

13

Goodyear blimp

Floating slowly across the sky, **blimps** look like huge balloons. They are filled with **helium** gas to make them float. Blimps have engines so they can be steered and **propelled.** The Goodyear blimp is one of the largest blimps flying today.

How big?
58.5 metres long

Hindenburg blimp

EXTREME FACT

The biggest blimp ever created was the Hindenburg. It was 245 metres long. The Hindenburg was destroyed by fire in 1937.

Nimitz aircraft carrier

The U.S. Navy's Nimitz **aircraft carriers** are huge. They can hold up to 85 aeroplanes on their decks. They carry aeroplanes all over the world. Each Nimitz aircraft carrier is longer than three football pitches.

How big?
333 metres long

17

Oasis cruise ship

Imagine a city floating in the middle of the sea. That is just what the cruise ship *Oasis of the Seas* feels like. This 16-deck ship carries over 6,000 **passengers**. Some *Oasis* cabins are as big as whole flats.

EXTREME FACT
This massive ship has a basketball court, a mini golf course, and two surfing machines!

How big?
361.7 metres long

Container ships

Some of the largest ships are container ships. They are used to carry goods across oceans in large containers, or boxes. The largest of them can carry 1.3 million televisions, or 50 million mobile phones!

Despite all the weight they carry, container ships still go at about 48 kph (30 mph).

How big?
335 metres long

Typhoon submarine

Russia's Typhoon **submarines** are the largest submarines in the world. The Typhoon submarines were feared for their quiet surprise attacks. Typhoon submarines can stay underwater for 120 days. They are currently used by the military for **missile** tests.

How big?
175 metres long

Tower crane

How are skyscrapers built? Giant cranes help do the job! A hook hangs from the end of the crane's long arm. The hook lifts heavy objects high in the air.

hook

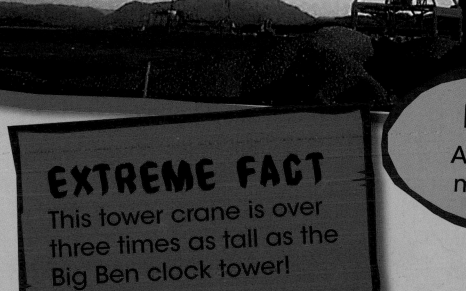

EXTREME FACT

This tower crane is over three times as tall as the Big Ben clock tower!

How big?
Almost 305 metres tall

The crawler-transporter

One of the largest land vehicles in the world is a crawler-transporter. They carry space rockets 8 kilometres, from the **assembly** building to the **launch pad**. They weigh 2,449 tonnes!

How big?
40 metres long and 34.7 metres wide

tracks

3
SIDE 3

Don't get your foot caught under these tracks!

27

Test yourself!

Try to match each question to the correct answer.

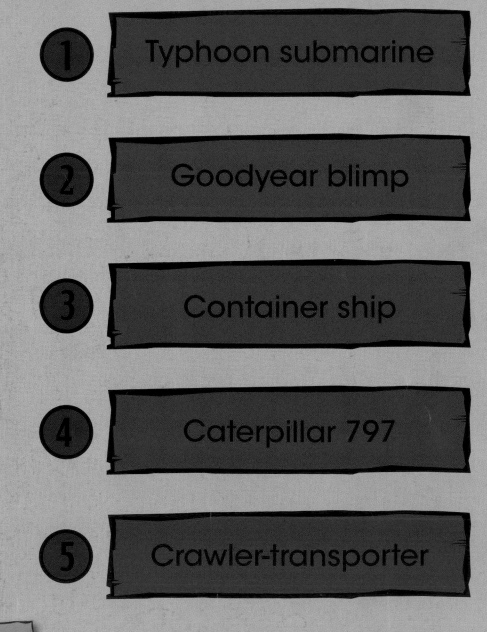

1. Typhoon submarine

2. Goodyear blimp

3. Container ship

4. Caterpillar 797

5. Crawler-transporter

Which machine transports rockets?

Which machine can stay underwater for 120 days?

Which machine is made for mining and construction projects?

Which machine can carry more than a million TVs?

Which machine is filled with helium gas?

Glossary

aircraft carrier large ship where military planes take off and land

assembly putting together of machine parts

blimp vehicle that floats through the air

construction act of building

helium gas that is lighter than air

launch pad place where space shuttles take off

mining digging rocks out of the ground

missile weapon for throwing or shooting

passenger person who travels in a car, bus, or other machine

propelled moved forward

submarine ship that travels underwater

Find out more

Find out

How tall is the crawler-transporter?

Books

Monster Trucks, Paul Harrison (Rosen Publishing Group, 2008)

Ships Up Close, Andra Abramson (Sterling Publishing, 2008)

Submarines and Submersibles, Kate Hayden (Dorling Kindersley, 2007)

Truck (Dorling Kindersley, 2007)

Websites

Bigfoot monster trucks
http://www.bigfoot4x4.com/
Includes pictures, videos, history and more about Bigfoot monster trucks.

Typhoon submarine
http://channel.nationalgeographic.com/series/ break-it-down/3859/Overview
Videos, photos, and facts about the Typhoon submarine.

NASA
http://science.ksc.nasa.gov/facilities/crawler.html
Includes pictures and detailed information about the crawler-transporter.

Index